HIGHEST PLACES ON THE PLANET

by Karen Soll

raintree

a Capstone company — publishers for children

Raintree is an imprint of Capstone Global Library Limited, a company incorporated in England and Wales having its registered office at 264 Banbury Road, Oxford, OX2 7DY – Registered company number: 6695582

www.raintree.co.uk
myorders@raintree.co.uk

Editorial Credits
Karen Soll, editor; Juliette Peters, designer;
Tracy Cummins, media specialist; Tori Abraham, production specialist

ISBN 978 1 4747 1265 1
20 19 18 17 16 15
10 9 8 7 6 5 4 3 2 1

British Library Cataloguing in Publication Data
A full catalogue record for this book is available from the British Library.

Photo Credits
Alamy: Urban Golob, 19; iStockphoto: Steve Krull, 9; Newscom: Harald von Radebrecht imageBROKER, 15; Shutterstock: Cristian Zamfir, Cover Top, Daniel Prudek, Design Element, 1, 21, Dominik Michalek, 5, Graeme Shannon, 13, Han Vu, 17, Ivsanmas, Map, Lenar Musin, Cover Bottom Right, LIUSHENGFILM, 11, Lukas Uher, 22, Michael Papasidero, 3, Vadim Petrakov, Cover Bottom Left, 7

Every effort has been made to contact copyright holders of material reproduced in this book. Any omissions will be rectified in subsequent printings if notice is given to the publisher.

All the internet addresses (URLs) given in this book were valid at the time of going to press. However, due to the dynamic nature of the internet, some addresses may have changed, or sites may have changed or ceased to exist since publication. While the author and publisher regret any inconvenience this may cause readers, no responsibility for any such changes can be accepted by either the author or the publisher.

Note to Parents and Teachers

The Extreme Earth set supports topics related to earth science. This book describes and illustrates climate and geography. The images support early readers in understanding the text. The repetition of words and phrases helps early readers learn new words. This book also introduces early readers to subject-specific vocabulary, which is defined in the Glossary section. Early readers may need assistance to read some words and to use the Table of contents, Glossary, Read more, Websites, Critical thinking questions, and Index sections of the book.

Printed and bound in China.

CONTENTS

HIGH PLACES

What would it be like
at the top of a mountain?
Let's find out about some of
the world's highest places.

Look up and see water
that falls a long way.
The world's highest waterfall
is called Angel Falls.
It is in South America.

Angel Falls in Venezuela is
979 metres (3,212 feet)
above sea level.

Leadville is in the Rocky Mountains.

It is also called Cloud City.

It is the highest city

in the United States.

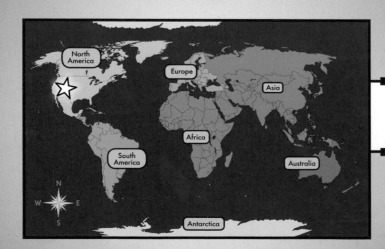

Leadville is 3,179 metres
(10,430 feet) above sea level.

HIGHER PLACES

People of the Tibet area
live on top of the world.
It is the highest place
people can live.

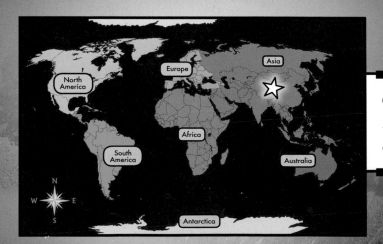

One village in Tibet is
5,099 metres (16,730 feet)
above sea level.

Kilimanjaro is

Africa's highest spot.

Its peak always has

snow and ice.

Kilimanjaro is 5,895 metres
(19,340 feet) above sea level.

HIGHEST PLACES

A volcano in South America formed a lake from rainwater. This is the highest lake.

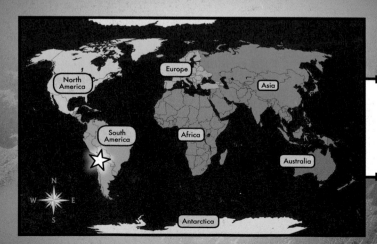

Licancábur volcano's lake is 5,916 metres (19,409 feet) above sea level.

Where is the highest mountain in North America? That is Mount McKinley.

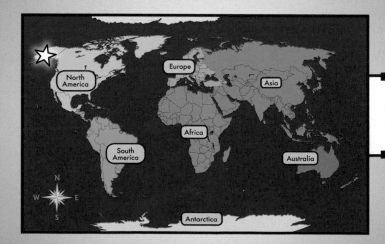

Mount McKinley is 6,194 metres (20,320 feet) above sea level.

The second highest spot
in the world is K2. K2 is
in Asia. The mountain is
rocky and snowy.

K2 is 8,611 metres (28,250 feet)
above sea level.

The highest spot in the world is Mount Everest. About 4,000 people have climbed it. The world has many high places. Which do you want to see?

Mount Everest is in the Himalayas. It is 8,850 metres (29,035 feet) above sea level.

GLOSSARY

area—a part

climb—to move upwards

mountain—a very tall piece of land, higher than a hill

peak—the pointed top of a mountain

Rocky Mountains—a major mountain range in western North America

sea level—the average level of the surface of the ocean, used as a starting point from which to measure the height or depth of any place

volcano—an opening in Earth's surface that sometimes sends out hot lava, steam and ash

waterfall—a place where river water falls from a high place to a lower place

READ MORE

Earth's Highest Places (Earth's Most Extreme Places), Mary Griffin (Gareth Stevens Publishing, 2015)

Harsh Habitats. (Extreme Nature), Anita Ganeri (Heinemann-Raintree, 2013)

Mountains (Natural Wonders), Kimberly M. Hutmacher, (Capstone Press, 2011)

WEBSITES

http://www.britannica.com/EBchecked/topic/1673089/Height-of-Mount-Everest

Visit this site to learn about attempts to measure Mount Everest.

http://education.nationalgeographic.com/education/encyclopedia/elevation/?ar_a=1

Discover what Mount Everest looks like from its peak.

http://www.factmonster.com/ipka/A0001763.html

Learn about some of the highest places in the world.

CRITICAL THINKING QUESTIONS

1. Why might Cloud City be a good nickname for Leadville?

2. Use the pictures and the text to compare Kilimanjaro to K2.

3. Pick one of the high places in this book. Write about what you might see there.

INDEX

Year: 2